THE JPS B'NAI MITZVAH TORAH COMMENTARY

Nitsavim (Deuteronomy 29:9–30:20)
Haftarah (Isaiah 61:10–63:9)

Rabbi Jeffrey K. Salkin

The Jewish Publication Society · Philadelphia
University of Nebraska Press · Lincoln

INTRODUCTION

News flash: the most important thing about becoming bar or bat mitzvah isn't the party. Nor is it the presents. Nor even being able to celebrate with your family and friends—as wonderful as those things are. Nor is it even standing before the congregation and reading the prayers of the liturgy—as important as that is.

No, the most important thing about becoming bar or bat mitzvah is sharing Torah with the congregation. And why is that? Because of all Jewish skills, that is the most important one.

Here is what is true about rites of passage: you can tell what a culture values by the tasks it asks its young people to perform on their way to maturity. In American culture, you become responsible for driving, responsible for voting, and yes, responsible for drinking responsibly.

In some cultures, the rite of passage toward maturity includes some kind of trial, or a test of strength. Sometimes, it is a kind of "outward bound" camping adventure. Among the Maasai tribe in Africa, it is traditional for a young person to hunt and kill a lion. In some Hispanic cultures, fifteen year-old girls celebrate the *quinceañera*, which marks their entrance into maturity.

What is Judaism's way of marking maturity? It combines both of these rites of passage: *responsibility* and *test*. You show that you are on your way to becoming a *responsible* Jewish adult through a public *test* of strength and knowledge—reading or chanting Torah, and then teaching it to the congregation.

This is the most important Jewish ritual mitzvah (commandment), and that is how you demonstrate that you are, truly, bar or bat mitzvah—old enough to be responsible for the mitzvot.

What Is Torah?

So, what exactly is the Torah? You probably know this already, but let's review.

The Torah (teaching) consists of "the five books of Moses," sometimes also called the *chumash* (from the Hebrew word *chameish,* which means "five"), or, sometimes, the Greek word Pentateuch (which means "the five teachings").

Here are the five books of the Torah, with their common names and their Hebrew names.

› **Genesis (The beginning), which in Hebrew is Bere'shit (from the first words—"When God began to create").** Bere'shit spans the years from Creation to Joseph's death in Egypt. Many of the Bible's best stories are in Genesis: the creation story itself; Adam and Eve in the Garden of Eden; Cain and Abel; Noah and the Flood; and the tales of the Patriarchs and Matriarchs, Abraham, Isaac, Jacob, Sarah, Rebekah, Rachel, and Leah. It also includes one of the greatest pieces of world literature, the story of Joseph, which is actually the oldest complete novel in history, comprising more than one-quarter of all Genesis.

› **Exodus (Getting out), which in Hebrew is Shemot (These are the names).** Exodus begins with the story of the Israelite slavery in Egypt. It then moves to the rise of Moses as a leader, and the Israelites' liberation from slavery. After the Israelites leave Egypt, they experience the miracle of the parting of the Sea of Reeds (or "Red Sea"); the giving of the Ten Commandments at Mount Sinai; the idolatry of the Golden Calf; and the design and construction of the Tabernacle and of the ark for the original tablets of the law, which our ancestors carried with them in the desert. Exodus also includes various ethical and civil laws, such as "You shall not wrong a stranger or oppress him, for you were strangers in the land of Egypt" (22:20).

› **Leviticus (about the Levites), or, in Hebrew, Va-yikra' (And God called).** It goes into great detail about the kinds of sacrifices that the ancient Israelites brought as offerings; the laws of ritual purity; the animals that were permitted and forbidden for eating (the beginnings of the tradition of kashrut, the Jewish dietary laws); the diagnosis of various skin diseases; the ethical laws of holiness; the ritual calendar of the Jewish year; and various agricultural laws concerning the treatment of the Land of Israel. Leviticus is basically the manual of ancient Judaism.

> Numbers (because the book begins with the census of the Israelites), or, in Hebrew, Be-midbar (In the wilderness). The book describes the forty years of wandering in the wilderness and the various rebellions against Moses. The constant theme: "Egypt wasn't so bad. Maybe we should go back." The greatest rebellion against Moses was the negative reports of the spies about the Land of Israel, which discouraged the Israelites from wanting to move forward into the land. For that reason, the "wilderness generation" must die off before a new generation can come into maturity and finish the journey.

> Deuteronomy (The repetition of the laws of the Torah), or, in Hebrew, Devarim (The words). The final book of the Torah is, essentially, Moses's farewell address to the Israelites as they prepare to enter the Land of Israel. Here we find various laws that had been previously taught, though sometimes with different wording. Much of Deuteronomy contains laws that will be important to the Israelites as they enter the Land of Israel—laws concerning the establishment of a monarchy and the ethics of warfare. Perhaps the most famous passage from Deuteronomy contains the *Shema,* the declaration of God's unity and uniqueness, and the *Ve-ahavta,* which follows it. Deuteronomy ends with the death of Moses on Mount Nebo as he looks across the Jordan Valley into the land that he will not enter.

Jews read the Torah in sequence—starting with Bere'shit right after Simchat Torah in the autumn, and then finishing Devarim on the following Simchat Torah. Each Torah portion is called a parashah (division; sometimes called a *sidrah,* a place in the order of the Torah reading). The stories go around in a full circle, reminding us that we can always gain more insights and more wisdom from the Torah. This means that if you don't "get" the meaning this year, don't worry—it will come around again.

And What Else? The Haftarah

We read or chant the Torah from the Torah scroll—the most sacred thing that a Jewish community has in its possession. The Torah is written without vowels, and the ability to read it and chant it is part of the challenge and the test.

But there is more to the synagogue reading. Every Torah reading has an accompanying haftarah reading. Haftarah means "conclusion," because there was once a time when the service actually ended with that reading. Some scholars believe that the reading of the haftarah originated at a time when non-Jewish authorities outlawed the reading of the Torah, and the Jews read the haftarah sections instead. In fact, in some synagogues, young people who become bar or bat mitzvah read very little Torah and instead read the entire haftarah portion.

The haftarah portion comes from the Nevi'im, the prophetic books, which are the second part of the Jewish Bible. It is either read or chanted from a Hebrew Bible, or maybe from a booklet or a photocopy.

The ancient sages chose the haftarah passages because their themes reminded them of the words or stories in the Torah text. Sometimes, they chose *haftarah* with special themes in honor of a festival or an upcoming festival.

Not all books in the prophetic section of the Hebrew Bible consist of prophecy. Several are historical. For example:

The book of Joshua tells the story of the conquest and settlement of Israel.

The book of Judges speaks of the period of early tribal rulers who would rise to power, usually for the purpose of uniting the tribes in war against their enemies. Some of these leaders are famous: Deborah, the great prophetess and military leader, and Samson, the biblical strong man.

The books of Samuel start with Samuel, the last judge, and then move to the creation of the Israelite monarchy under Saul and David (approximately 1000 BCE).

The books of Kings tell of the death of King David, the rise of King Solomon, and how the Israelite kingdom split into the Northern Kingdom of Israel and the Southern Kingdom of Judah (approximately 900 BCE).

And then there are the books of the prophets, those spokesmen for God whose words fired the Jewish conscience. Their names are immortal: Isaiah, Jeremiah, Ezekiel, Amos, Hosea, among others.

Someone once said: "There is no evidence of a biblical prophet ever being invited back a second time for dinner." Why? Because the prophets were tough. They had no patience for injustice, apathy, or hypocrisy. No one escaped their criticisms. Here's what they taught:

> God commands the Jews to behave decently toward one another. In fact, God cares more about basic ethics and decency than about ritual behavior.
> God chose the Jews *not* for special privileges, but for special duties to humanity.
> As bad as the Jews sometimes were, there was always the possibility that they would improve their behavior.
> As bad as things might be now, it will not always be that way. Someday, there will be universal justice and peace. Human history is moving forward toward an ultimate conclusion that some call the Messianic Age: a time of universal peace and prosperity for the Jewish people and for all the people of the world.

Your Mission—To Teach Torah to the Congregation

On the day when you become bar or bat mitzvah, you will be reading, or chanting, Torah—in Hebrew. You will be reading, or chanting, the haftarah—in Hebrew. That is the major skill that publicly marks the becoming of bar or bat mitzvah. But, perhaps even more important than that, you need to be able to teach something about the Torah portion, and perhaps the haftarah as well.

And that is where this book comes in. It will be a very valuable resource for you, and your family, in the b'nai mitzvah process.

Here is what you will find in it:

> A brief **summary** of every Torah portion. This is a basic overview of the portion; and, while it might not refer to everything in the Torah portion, it will explain its most important aspects.
> A list of the **major ideas** in the Torah portion. The purpose: to make the Torah portion real, in ways that we can relate to. Every Torah portion contains unique ideas, and when you put all

of those ideas together, you actually come up with a list of Judaism's most important ideas.

› Two ***divrei Torah*** ("words of Torah," or "sermonettes") for each portion. These *divrei Torah* explain significant aspects of the Torah portion in accessible, reader-friendly language. Each *devar Torah* contains references to **traditional** Jewish sources (those that were written before the modern era), as well as **modern** sources and quotes. We have searched, far and wide, to find sources that are unusual, interesting, and not just the "same old stuff" that many people already know about the Torah portion. Why did we include these minisermons in the volume? Not because we want you to simply copy those sermons and pass them off as your own (that would be cheating), though you are free to quote from them. We included them so that you can see what is possible—how you can try to make meaning for yourself out of the words of Torah.

› **Connections:** This is perhaps the most valuable part. It's a list of questions that you can ask yourself, or that others might help you think about—any of which can lead to the creation of your *devar Torah.*

Note: you don't have to like everything that's in a particular Torah portion. Some aren't that loveable. Some are hard to understand; some are about religious practices that people today might find confusing, and even offensive; some contain ideas that we might find totally outmoded.

But this doesn't have to get in the way. After all, most kids spend a lot of time thinking about stories that contain ideas that modern people would find totally bizarre. Any good medieval fantasy story falls into that category.

And we also believe that, if you spend just a little bit of time with those texts, you can begin to understand what the author was trying to say.

This volume goes one step further. Sometimes, the haftarah comes off as a second thought, and no one really thinks about it. We have tried to solve that problem by including a **summary** of each haftarah, and then a mini-sermon on the haftarah. This will help you learn how these sacred words are relevant to today's world, and even to your own life.

All Bible quotations come from the NJPS translation, which is found in the many different editions of the JPS TANAKH; in the Conservative movement's *Etz Hayim: Torah and Commentary;* in the Reform movement's *Torah: A Modern Commentary;* and in other Bible commentaries and study guides.

How Do I Write a *Devar Torah?*

It really is easier than it looks.

There are many ways of thinking about the *devar Torah.* It is, of course, a short sermon on the meaning of the Torah (and, perhaps, the haftarah) portion. It might even be helpful to think of the *devar Torah* as a "book report" on the portion itself.

The most important thing you can know about this sacred task is: *Learn* the words. *Love* the words. Teach people what it could mean to *live* the words.

Here's a basic outline for a *devar Torah:*

"My Torah portion is (name of portion) _____,
    from the book of _____, chapter
    _____.

"In my Torah portion, we learn that_____
    (Summary of portion)
"For me, the most important lesson of this Torah portion is (what
    is the best thing in the portion? Take the portion as a whole;
    your *devar Torah* does not have to be only, or specifically, on the
    verses that you are reading).
"As I learned my Torah portion, I found myself wondering:
    ➤ *Raise a question that the Torah portion itself raises.*
    ➤ *"Pick a fight"* with the portion. Argue with it.
    ➤ *Answer a question* that is listed in the "Connections" section of
      each Torah portion.
    ➤ *Suggest a question to your rabbi* that you would want the rabbi
      to answer in his or her own *devar Torah* or sermon.

"I have lived the values of the Torah by _____
(here, you can talk about how the Torah portion relates to your
own life. If you have done a mitzvah project, you can talk about
that here).

How To Keep It from Being Boring
(and You from Being Bored)

Some people just don't like giving traditional speeches. From our perspective, that's really okay. Perhaps you can teach Torah in a different way—one that makes sense to you.

› Write an "open letter" to one of the characters in your Torah portion. "Dear Abraham: I hope that your trip to Canaan was not too hard . . ." "Dear Moses: Were you afraid when you got the Ten Commandments on Mount Sinai? I sure would have been . . ."
› Write a news story about what happens. Imagine yourself to be a television or news reporter. "Residents of neighboring cities were horrified yesterday as the wicked cities of Sodom and Gomorrah were burned to the ground. Some say that God was responsible . . ."
› Write an imaginary interview with a character in your Torah portion.
› Tell the story from the point of view of another character, or a minor character, in the story. For instance, tell the story of the Garden of Eden from the point of view of the serpent. Or the story of the Binding of Isaac from the point of view of the ram, which was substituted for Isaac as a sacrifice. Or perhaps the story of the sale of Joseph from the point of view of his coat, which was stripped off him and dipped in a goat's blood.
› Write a poem about your Torah portion.
› Write a song about your Torah portion.
› Write a play about your Torah portion, and have some friends act it out with you.
› Create a piece of artwork about your Torah portion.

The bottom line is: Make this a joyful experience. Yes—it could even be fun.

The Very Last Thing You Need to Know at This Point

The Torah scroll is written without vowels. Why? Don't *sofrim* (Torah scribes) know the vowels?

Of course they do.

So, why do they leave the vowels out?

One reason is that the Torah came into existence at a time when sages were still arguing about the proper vowels, and the proper pronunciation.

But here is another reason: The Torah text, as we have it today, and as it sits in the scroll, is actually *an unfinished work*. Think of it: the words are just sitting there. Because they have no vowels, it is as if they have no voice.

When we read the Torah publicly, we give voice to the ancient words. And when we find meaning in those ancient words, and we talk about those meanings, those words jump to life. They enter our lives. They make our world deeper and better.

Mazal tov to you, and your family. This is your journey toward Jewish maturity. Love it.

THE TORAH

❖ Nitsavim: Deuteronomy 29:9–30:20

Time is running out for Moses. This Torah portion, which is often com-
bined with the next parashah, Va-yelekh, contains the crucial speech that
Moses delivers on the very last day of his life, and he is feeling a sense of
urgency. As the Israelites stand on the steppes of Moab, preparing to enter the Land of Israel, Moses reminds them that it is not only they who
are standing there, entering into the covenant, but also all future Jews.

Moses reserves a special contempt for those who would turn away
from God and the covenant. But Moses also reminds them that those
who turn away can always turn back. Unwilling to allow his final
words to be filled with anger, Moses encourages the Israelites and
helps them understand that the covenant is not too difficult to follow,
and that the Torah presents them with choices—life or death, blessing
or curse. When all is said and done, the Israelites must "choose life."

Summary

- Moses tells the Israelites that they all stand before God, and that they stand before God equally, without regard to age, gender, and the kind of work that they do. God makes the covenant not only with them, but also with those "who are not with us here this day." (29:9–13)
- Moses warns against those who continue to worship idols. He condemns the way that those idol worshipers think about what they are doing—thinking only about themselves and not about the rest of the community. It is that kind of selfish thinking that deserves terrible punishments. (29:15–27)
- As bad as things might get with the Jewish people—no matter how much they sin and are punished with exile—Moses reassures them that, ultimately, God will take them back in love, and bring them back to the Land of Israel. (30:1–10)
- Moses reminds the people that *teshuvah* is not only necessary, it is possible. The Torah is not too hard for people to do. Nevertheless, they still have a choice: between life and death, and blessing and curse. All God can do is ask them to make the right choice. (30:11–20)

The Big Ideas

- **Judaism is never only about "now." It is also about the future.** This is perhaps one of Deuteronomy's greatest messages: a focus on the education of children, and the sense that the Jewish people must endure into the future. We might even say that Deuteronomy introduces the idea of a Jewish future. Moreover, the covenant with God is meant to be inclusive—men, women, children, menial laborers, even non-Jews who live in the midst of the Jewish community.

- **The individual Jew can never think only about himself or herself.** True, Moses condemns those who still worship the idols of the surrounding nations. That is bad enough, but what really gets Moses angry is those who think that they will get away with idol worship and that they can do whatever they want. In this way, Moses is being more than a little prophetic. To this day, there are Jews who only think about themselves and not about the implications of their actions for the Jewish people or on the Jewish future. They are following their "own willful heart." Moses warns that this attitude, if it continues, will ultimately destroy the Jewish people, and that God ultimately knows what goes on in the privacy of people's lives.

- **Without *teshuvah*, Judaism and the Jewish people could not exist.** Of all the Jewish ideas that originated in Deuteronomy—the love of God, education of subsequent generations, the ability to make moral and spiritual choices, the emphasis on social justice—perhaps the most important one is *teshuvah*. It is often translated as "repentance," but it really means "return." In this particular case in the Torah portion, it means that if the Jews repent they will be able to return from exile to the Land of Israel. In fact, the verb *shuv,* "to return," appears more often in this Torah portion than in the entire Torah. It is hardly a coincidence that this portion is always the one that is read in the synagogue right before the beginning of the Days of Awe. *Teshuvah,* the main theme of the High Holy Days, is written all over it.

➤ **Judaism is doable.** Judaism is not a secret teaching that only a comparatively few people can figure out. Neither is it overburdened with difficult ritual practices that just the extremely dedicated can perform. It is for all Jews. But God cannot force us to perform the mitzvot. Neither can God force us to do *teshuvah* and return to the right way of living. Those are choices that only we can make.

Divrei Torah

YOU CAN DO IT!

"I can't do it. . . . It's too hard!" How many times have you said that, either to yourself or to others? Perhaps it was a new move or skill in a sport. Perhaps a challenging piece of music. Maybe it was having to move to a new home with your family, or starting at a new camp. Maybe it was learning Hebrew. Whatever it is, we all come up against things that seem to be really hard for us to do.

What about Judaism?

There is a hint of that in this Torah portion, too. Moses tells the People of Israel: "Surely, this Instruction which I enjoin upon you this day is not too baffling for you, nor is it beyond reach" (30:11).

Which mitzvah (commandment) is Moses talking about? If you look at what the passage is talking about immediately before Moses delivers these words of encouragement, you might think that the subject is *teshuvah*, "repentance" or "return."

Moses is saying that the mitzvah of repentance is not too hard for someone to do. And this might well be a surprise to us, because if you've ever been in a position of having to say that you are sorry to someone, or (even harder) having to dig down deep inside yourself and say, "I could be better," or, if you've ever had to reconsider an idea that you first thought was great or had to deal with regrets about something, you know how hard it can be.

But perhaps the mitzvah that the verse is referring to is not the mitzvah of *teshuvah* at all. Perhaps the mitzvah is all the mitzvot—all of Judaism itself.

If this is so, then the verse is teaching us that it's not impossible to understand Judaism and follow its laws and teachings, or to practice Judaism. You don't have to go into the heavens to retrieve Judaism's real meaning. A midrash puts it this way: "Moses told the Israelites that he was not going to bring them another Torah from heaven. Nothing of it has remained in heaven." It is all there, right in front of you. It is real. It is doable.

Jewish observance poses challenges. It's not easy to observe Shabbat in any real and meaningful way; it requires doing certain things (like rituals) and not doing certain things. The same thing is true of kashrut. It can be a challenge to figure out what and how to eat, and that can make going to restaurants difficult; but as generations of Jews will tell you, it is doable. Fasting on Yom Kippur: hard, but doable. Learning Hebrew: sometimes hard, but quite often doable (some people just can't learn a foreign language, no matter how hard they try). And no matter how hard the mitzvot are, throughout history Jews have often sacrificed their lives in order to do them.

Says Bible scholar Avivah Zornberg: "God is like a very patient piano teacher who is constantly introducing us to new ways of playing the sacred music. God doesn't give us any pieces that are too hard for our playing level."

The commandments. Hard? Yes. Too hard? No. Their worth? Priceless!

DO IT TODAY!

Don't you find it irritating when people keep using the same words, over and over again? Some people just have their favorite words or clichés, and, frankly, they can get a little annoying.

That is how Moses was with the word *ha-yom,* "today" or "this day." Moses uses it five times in 29:9–17, and then, again, another seven times in 30:1–19. "You stand this day" (29:9); and then again in 29:12: "to the end that He may establish you this day as His people": and then again in 30:2: "just as I enjoin upon you this day." And then, again in 30:11: "Surely, this Instruction which I enjoin upon you this day." You get the idea.

Why this constant repetition of "today?" In the words of the great medieval commentator Rashi: "This teaches that Moses, on the day of his death, gathered them together before God to bring them into the covenant." Moses is delivering this speech on the final day of his life. "Today," "this day," has very special meaning for him. If Moses did not get this sacred work done *ha-yom,* today, it would not get done.

But, maybe Moses was not simply referring to "today" or "this day" as the particular day when he spoke. Perhaps Moses meant that whenever we read these words we should think of those words being delivered "today"—on the very day that we read them. After all, Moses made the covenant "not with you alone, but both with those who are standing here with us this day . . . and with those who are not here with us this day" (29:13). That's all of us.

Imagine, then, a Jewish science fiction movie in which all time is collapsed. Past, present, and future no longer exist. The late comedian George Carlin once said: "Time is just God's way of making sure that everything doesn't happen all at once." In fact, this is how Jewish ritual works. Every time we read the Torah, it is as if we ourselves are standing on Mount Sinai, or in Moab, becoming part of the covenant. Every time we sit at the Passover seder, it is as if we ourselves are getting out of Egypt. (Some Jews even act out the Exodus at the seder itself—getting up from the table and going outside the house.) At a Jewish wedding, the couple "becomes" Adam and Eve in the Garden of Eden—the first couple in history.

In the words of the contemporary scholar Everett Fox: "'Today' in this Torah portion challenges all hearers of the text to make the moment their own. The book of Deuteronomy, the great example of the Teaching made new, thus begins the Jewish process, as old as the Bible itself, of rehearing and rethinking the tradition."

One last thing about "today." As you get older, you will probably figure this out. Laziness is an unattractive quality. So is procrastination—putting things off. Especially when it comes to observing the commandments and doing good deeds, making amends, honoring your parents, reaching out to friends, paying attention to your grandparents—don't put it off. Do it today!

CONNECTIONS

> What can you do to contribute to the Jewish future?
> Do you believe that Jewish education is important? How can you demonstrate your commitment to Jewish learning?
> In what ways have you shown your commitment to the larger Jewish community?
> Have you ever done *teshuvah* (repented, asked for forgiveness) for something that you've done? What was that experience like? How did it feel?
> Are there things that you once thought were difficult that have actually proven to be either easy or, at least, doable?
> What are some things that you keep putting off? How can you break yourself of that habit?

THE HAFTARAH

❖ Nitsavim: Isaiah 61:10–63:9

This haftarah has a double name because it's read along with two *parshiyot,* Nitsavim and Va-yelekh.

Seven weeks ago, it was Tisha b'Av. The Babylonians destroyed Jerusalem and the Temple. The horror was beyond imagining. (Read the book of Lamentations for the eyewitness accounts; it is not pretty.)

For seven weeks, Jews have been reading *haftarot* that ask the following questions: Can God bring us home from Babylon? *Will* God bring us home from Babylon? And the answer is: Yes. Yes, it is time to come home. And this is no mere "coming home." It's like a wedding in which God is the bridegroom and Israel is the bride. "Like a bridegroom adorned with a turban, like a bride bedecked with her finery" (61:10).

More than that: sometimes, when people get married, the bride will take a new name—usually, her husband's last name. (This happens less often these days, but it's still common.) When the Jewish people "marry" God, it's not as if God has a last name for them to take (!). But they do change their names—"Nevermore shall you be called 'Forsaken,' nor shall your land be called 'Desolate'; but you shall be called 'I delight in her,' and your land 'Espoused'" (62:4).

In the Bible, when someone's name is changed—for example, Abram to Abraham, Sarai to Sarah, Jacob to Israel—it means a total change of status. And that is what has happened to the Jewish people. Changing their name, even poetically and temporarily, means that they have changed their status from a demoralized people to a victorious people. Or, think of it this way: there is an old Jewish custom to change the name of someone who is seriously ill, imagining that this will confuse the Angel of Death. The Jewish people have been seriously "ill," suffering from inner despair. So, change their name—let them live again!

When It Comes to Israel, Don't Be Silent

If you were going to look for the verse from the haftarah that has had the most enduring influence, it would be this one: "For the sake of Zion I will not be silent; for the sake of Jerusalem I will not be still, till her victory emerge resplendent and her triumph like a flaming torch" (62:1).

The great Bible commentator Rashi, who lived in the Middle Ages, didn't forget what that verse means. In fact, he had a new understanding of it, because he lived in the days of the Crusades, when armies went to war in Jerusalem: "I shall act, and I shall not be silent about what was done to Jerusalem, and I will not be at peace until her victory emerges."

But, nowadays, what does it mean not to be silent regarding Zion? It means recognizing that Israel is the ancestral home of the Jewish people, and it is part of every Jew's religious identity. It means recognizing that Israel is a refuge from antisemitism, and that it is a place where Jews can go to escape persecution and be safe. Finally, it means recognizing that Israel is an example to the rest of the world for how to engage in *tikkun olam,* repairing the world.

What can you do to support Israel, and to speak up with your own deeds? You can visit Israel; make friends with Israelis and stay in touch with them; improve your knowledge of Hebrew; follow what's happening in the Israeli political arena; buy Israeli products whenever possible, especially food products; write letters to the newspaper supporting and defending Israel; give *tzedakah* to organizations that support Israel; read Israeli newspapers and magazines online; read books about Israel; listen to Israeli rock music; watch Israeli films; follow Israeli sports; learn to cook Israeli or Middle Eastern dishes.

And why should Jews not be silent about Israel? Think about how the Jews in Babylon felt. They had been dreaming about returning to the Land of Israel; now it is becoming a reality. So, too, with modern Jews, who especially after the Holocaust could celebrate a return to the Jewish homeland.

As the late Esther Jungreis writes about her childhood in a Nazi concentration camp: "The nights in Bergen Belsen were very long. I would close my eyes and try to escape by recalling stories from the Bible, stories of our sages, and stories of Jerusalem. We would yet come to Jerusalem, where the sun always shone, where no one ever went hungry, where, my mother assured me, candy bars actually grew on trees, and birds sang the psalms of King David. Never had a nation returned to its land after two thousand years, and we saw it with our very eyes. The ancient prophecy was fulfilled."

How can one be silent or apathetic about the miracle by the Mediterranean that is Israel?

CPSIA information can be obtained
at www.ICGtesting.com
Printed in the USA
LVHW091832250319
611761LV00003B/405/P